He Loved Me Beyond My Thong

LayFayette Nicci Jackson-Steward

He Loved Me Beyond My Thong

LayFayette Nicci Jackson Steward

Copyright © 2018

All rights reserved. No part of this publication may be reproduced, distributed, or transmitted in any form or by any means, including photocopying, recording, or other electronic or mechanical methods, without the prior written permission of the publisher, except in the case of brief quotations embodied in critical reviews and certain other noncommercial uses permitted by copyright law. For permission requests, write to the publisher, addressed "Attention: Permissions Coordinator," at the address below.

Truth Seeker Publishing
7611 South Broadway
St Louis, Mo 63111

Truthseekers.publishing@yahoo.com

1-800-728-9561

Truth Seeker Publishing

Ordering Information:

Quantity sales. Special discounts are available on quantity purchases by corporations, associations, and others. For details, contact the publisher at the address above.

Orders by U.S. trade bookstores and wholesalers.

ISBN-13:
978-1720687597

ISBN-10:
1720687595

Printed in the United States of America

DEDICATION

First giving honor to the Lord God and Jesus Christ his son. He is the reason for my being no matter what. (John 3:16)

To my family and friends near and far. To my Pastors.

To my helper and friend Kimberly Fulton I give a very special thanks because she has been walking out her new found life in Christ and she recognized her purpose. She doesn't mind helping and motivating others. She motivated me by telling me to do what God said do. To all who will be blessed by me telling my testimony and the things I went through.

Thank you to everyone who has helped me along the way.

Layfayette Nicci Jackson-Steward

ABOUT THE TITLE

When I started on writing this book, the name of the book was Eve Bit the Apple Will You Too? The second title was Lips of Fire on me. I heard the Lord say I loved you beyond your Thong. The revelation I got was Lord you love me past me. Lord you have loved me beyond any failures, disappointments, and anytime I may have grieved you. Thank you Lord for loving me.

LIPS OF FIRE

I have to give thanks to my Almighty God because if it wasn't for him I would not be here (John 3:16, 17). I have been blessed with up and downs learning to deal with life issues and how to overcome others attitudes and behavior.

You will meet people that will like and will not like you, it's still up to you to overcome and stand up for what you believe in and who is your God Lord and Savior.

Now I have my children in my life that gives me a run for my money and lessons on life also. In the process of writing this book my son Daray says what are you writing and I said a book then he said who letter and I said from Trojan to me. Daray says ok you writing another episode to the movie The Best Man Holiday, if he put you across a balcony l am gone to be Julian and stand back looking like is he really. I just busted out laughing because he looked like he was so for real, kids can say some of the craziest things at times. Well to say my daughter Denasia not having it she's gone have my back.

How do you go through life without giving honor also to my parents, children James, Daray and Denasia .siblings, cousins, friends, frenemies, teachers, pastors, my church family, the law, and the things that are to come? So I will say thank you and I love all of you for the experience I have had and most of all coming into the knowledge of the Lord Jesus Christ.

Love you

LayFayette Nicci Jackson-Steward

Layfayette Nicci Jackson-Steward

There is no greater love than Jesus Christ.

There's a man that loves better than this world will ever give you. I can show enough be a witness on learning a lessons on everything now. Oh how you can love someone and they can turn on you, hurt and leave you? Is that how God, feels when we turn away from him to please ourselves this flesh? Serving other things and not him but God still loves us and waiting for us to turn from our mess repenting saying I/we need you Father. You are the head of our lives I/we submit my will to do your will, I will not turn away from you again, I will stay and bare my cross no matter how hard the trails get I will stay (Luke 14:27).

I know I must die to the flesh daily to be able to abide in you and you abide in me (1 Corinthians 15:31 John 15:4). I must refuse to fall to my old ways of sin, I can't do it by myself I need Your hand on me I can't do nothing in me I only fool myself if I do. I must repent to my ways that are not yours. I will rejoice in your Father, I will bless your name all the time (Psalm34). I had to learn to STOP trying to be sexed or so-called loved and read who loves me/you unconditional, 1st giving himself for me/you so that we can be free and have life more abundantly(John 10) dying for our sins.

I AM the rose of Shar'-on, and the Lily of the Valley. As the lily among thorns, so is my love among the daughters.

As the apple tree among the trees of the woods, so is my beloved among the sons. I sat down under his shadow with great delight, and his fruit was sweet to my taste. He brought me to the banqueting house, and his banner over me was love (Song of Solomon 2).

Finding the love that only God can fill in me and learning of his ultimate love for me is more for filling than a rushing ride on a roller coaster and how he gives us revelation of him. I just want to please him in all my days and thank him for blessing me with this life he gave me. Thank you so much Father thank you so much for loving me like no other.

I give all honor to the head of my life.

My Lord

My Father

My God

My Lord Jesus Christ

The main goal of this book is to educate single women and men on the pitfalls of dating and attaching themselves to the wrong person. I intend to give you some red flags to look out for. In this journey you need to beware and to watch for red flags. Be aware and listen to how someone approaches you and speaks to you. Just because someone is telling you I Love you doesn't necessarily mean that they do.

1. Learn who you are dating before you commit.

2. The wrong boo can beat, take, drain or kill you.

3. Don't let anyone charm your soul to hell.

4. We have fallen away from foundational morals and truths.

5. Be rooted in Jesus and he will give you the right Boaz or Ruth.

6. The word says a **he who finds a wife finds a good thing and obtains the favor of the Lord.** Proverbs 18:22

7. Love Jesus first and he will give you a mate. (Don't go looking without the Holy Ghost leading)

Just be careful who you let whisper sweet nothings in your ears.

LIPS OF FIRE

REASONS WHY.

1. Words can hurt.
2. The wrong way to fall in love can make you happy or bitter.
3. Watch what or who you listen to.
4. Falling for the wrong one can leave you scared.
5. Who or what will you believe?
6. Watch who talking in your ears.
7. Listening to the wrong one can tear you into.
8. Who do you have in your ears?
9. Falling in love with the wrong A**'s.
10. The wrong Bo can whip your Yazz to.
11. What is your season Part-time, no time or my lifetime?
12. There's a reason, season or lifetime that people comes in your life we have to seek to know which one and not to hold anyone past their time.
13. I was told by my aunt don't be any fool for them and don't let them piss on you and call it rain.
14. You tried me like Billy Joe lunchmeat daughter.
15. Go ahead and jump Amtrak and make me derail not today.
16. To tell me half of the truth is just a whole lie.

Layfayette Nicci Jackson-Steward

MY POEM

The pain for the rain

The tears for the fears we need not have

The test..... War for the test we will endure

The overflowing of his amazing grace we take for granted

For the croak we get in the throat at the moment of tragedy

It hurts so..........

But I could never know what he did for me on that cross

I don't belong to myself

Psalm 37:3-8

Trust in the LORD, and do good; dwell in the land, and feed on His faithfulness.

Delight thyself also in the LORD, and he shall give thee the desires of thine heart.

Commit thy way unto the LORD; Trust also in Him, And He shall bring it to pass.

Rest in the LORD, and wait patiently for Him; do not fret because of him, who prospers in his way,

Cease from anger, and forsake wrath; do not fret- it only causes harm.

I KNOW WHO I AM

I am 5'5. 230 plus pounds 6'9 in the Lord Now what do you want to do. The only thing I would change about me is my age and weight I laugh at how they try me and I can pray for them. It's just nasty to me how guys try you and don't care. How you want to be a whore sleeping with everyone not me. The only spare tire around me is in my car. No I do not need a sugar daddy to pay my bills. No I don't do married men. No I will not send nude pictures to you. No you can't come to my house just to chill, watch Tv and eat my food. God is good. When he want you to stay saved. The guy I was seeing was seeing others also. Their emails came to me. Cheaters can be so dumb at times. I was calling him the Boo name he was calling himself to her.

I have learned to let something that have happened in my past to stay in my past. It caused major damage. Stay in the Word. Wait on the voice of God to lead you to God. Don't do things in your feelings. You will get the wrong signal. You will think it's the lord and it's the enemy. Fall in love with Jesus with your whole heart. Seek his kingdom and he will supply your needs. (Philippians 4:19).

I know my bloopers and how good God's grace and mercy is. Don't get caught and grace runs out on you. A saying don't get caught up the river without a paddle.

Being single and truly saved, running for God is more fulfilling to me than going to hell. It is not in my time but God's timming. Its not about me, but God.

CHAPTER ONE

    I met Trojan back about eighteen years ago in the apartments where my mother lived. He had a crush on me and I had a little one for him but we didn't take it anywhere. We talked trash to each other all the time, time flew by and we moved away. I knew Trojan's family and I would see them from time to time. On this sad occasion when I did see Trojan it was because his mother had passed away. It's the first of August two-thousand twenty fourteen when we did go eye to eye after two minutes. Trojan said you know we should have been married after all that play auguring we did then. We just busted out laughing.

    What I knew of Trojan that he had one child, and he was constantly in and out of relationships. He worked but had made bad choices at times hustling in the streets and was sent to prison. Trojan was released from prison to attend his mother funeral.

    While we were in the car together with his sister driving to take him back to the prison, we were laughing and making jokes about being married and how we can have puppies and the puppies give us little grand puppies. In a roundabout way he asked me to write him by saying a stamp only cost forty-two cents. So one day I sent him a letter.

My First Letter

    Thinking to myself a couple of days after seeing Trojan what if God sent him to me because I wasn't looking for anyone at the time.

I know that the Bible tells me that a man that findeth a wife findeth a good thing (Proverbs 18). it has been two years of me being single before I saw Trojan again.

Not sure what to say and you asked me to write you so that's what I'm doing. I don't know what all I said it is the first letter, letting him know I gave up my bottle of tea to write him and hope he is feeling better. Giving him scriptures from the Bible about to put God first and to pray and just believe what the word of God says and that the pain of losing his mother not to hold that in she's gone but she is with God.

I won't give his real name I will just call him Trojan and myself Rainiee.

Trojan: What's up Boo I'm just responding to your letter? I'm glad to see that you're one of God's children. I didn't know that, the way you be talking you should be preaching or something. I try to stay right, I'm just a work in progress. I take it day by day. It's just that I am fighting against myself, the pain I feel sometimes is more than I can bare and then I think about God's word, He will not put any more on you than you can bare. I wonder about that sometimes, here I am barely making it up and down, in my happiness and sadness hoping maybe one person would think damn maybe my brother would like a letter or something. I wonder how my life got so Fu** up. I'm just glad the Lord, keeps waking me up to get it right. Well enough about my sad self, how are you doing and are the kids and family well? I'm so depressed right now it's hard for me to write any poems, I got to get out of this depression. I got to pray and let God, take care of it. But other than that I'm still living and that's what counts right.

Let me see part-one this is called The One (poem)

You know I am looking around me.

As I was walking down the street,

I saw her and my heart skipped a beat and I said damn is this the one.

The one that's in my dreams, the one that gives me joy, the one face that hunts my dreams.

Then I see her face: her beauty was like a rose blooming in the summer on a spring day. Her body was fine, her eyes were the color of the sweetest light brown.

Is this the one or is it a cruel joke someone is playing?

Then I chase behind her damn is "Is this the one is this the one".

CHAPTER TWO

Trojan: Hey Boo let me start out by saying that I enjoyed your letter now I hope this letter reaches you and your family in good health☺. I have learned to love the small things and take time out to see all God's, things he created the stars I just love looking at.

I guess you bring out the best in me, oh SH** I should not have said that because I'm trying to really know you. I think people should become friends before other things happen☺. That has been my problem all the time not getting to know a person before we take things further. I'm going to take me time and move really slow, I'm trying to choose my queen and she can't just be anybody. First she has to love God, before anybody else you already have that in you ☺ she has to be funny and have a sense of humor but also she has to be strong and has good values and a love for the family you know anybody like that☺.

To be a better man, trust God, taking more steps to become what God, has always wanted me to be mostly. I'm just trying to stay one step ahead of them busters getting a job is most important right now. That's the key save my money and gets my own place; be at a place in life when I'm ready to go somewhere I can, not living from paycheck to paycheck.

So would you like to go somewhere and dance I have the perfect place but I'm not going to tell you where because I want to be the one to take you. So put on your dancing shoes and let's party, I hope

I can get a slow dance here and there because I'm not too good with that hip hop junk.

Until then Dear God you know I will give my very best.

I just want the chance to take you out and put a smile on your face, like a long walk on the beach and get you on the dance floor and let you have a good time. To go see that funny movie you like, dreams baby dreams and if you dream enough sometimes they come true and this is from a man that just wants to make you smile. And I just want to say thank you Boo be bless and wait.

Rainiee: Not much besides church and I go to the park to watch the sun glare on the water while the birds fly past. I go to visit family every other weekend. Movies I like are funny not all that cursing or sex scenes clean cut cartoons, clean action movies. I don't do scary movies, family ones are great. I play around with the kids with dancing have not been to the club since I became saved. You have to know a person mind and love it before you have the body.

By reading from what Trojan sent me you can just about put two & two together on what we talked about, I only had the letters he wrote to me, I tried to match up what I said by what he had written back to me much as possible.

Well tell me more about yourself. If I knew this was going to happen: I would have kept the notes that the other guy *Rufus gave me about how I was the apple of his eye and his queen*. Well to tell a little about Rufus my middle school crush, my itchy ears listening to him filling my head with them sweet mind-blowing dreams that he know I'm the woman for him I'm his wife. Rufus went around telling almost everyone even went to my parents and ask can he marry me and I'm thirty-eight years old. Oh how charming is that at my age for a guy to ask my parents for your hand in marriage? Who would not want a man to sweep them off their feet? Well this brother sold me a plain without the engine had me going for a moment until his true colors open my eyes. Why am I writing this book because the flesh is a mess? It may feel good at that time but it became the most disgusting feeling ever. To be touched by a man, you can be in a relationship and be raped no means no who was gone to believe he raped me, who was I gone to tell the shame I was feeling because I was shaking up and going to church.

Well listen to me somewhere I missed God in this because Rufus was a walking two leg full of words just to win his way in and use you. This is bound to happen when you are not in Gods covering. I'm thankful that Jesus loved me just that much to bring me out of my mess and saved me from losing my life and children. This trail opened my eyes and made me stronger in the Lord showing me that I have to wait my time, seeking God while I wait first. This flesh is a dirty mess got me thinking that I need a man at times, I could have been exposed to drugs or got a disease from Rufus but the hands of God kept me.

Yes we all fall short into sin which if we choose to stay it becomes an iniquity, we need to get up and repent and call on

the name of Jesus. We live around sin every day we have to stand firm and refuse to let the flesh win only in the blood of Jesus we can do it, nothing we can do in ourselves. I step out in my flesh to live with this man, unmarried and the conviction I received from God drove me to get it right and to see the side of sleeping with the enemy will cost you. I felt off in two-thousand and eleven. Now that I'm thinking about it when we tell the story from the Bible that's what happen by Satan used an apple to trick Eve.

Trojan: Hey Boo, You said you want to know about me, well I'm just a normal guy I love to have fun tell jokes *I love the Lord very much, every day I get better at being what he wants me to be. I like for people to be honest with me because if you lie you have to keep covering up things, I learned long time ago just to be real, and I hate all that lying.* I'm a homebody I like to come home from work and chill with my lady watching movies and stuff can't get in trouble that way.

I'm a one woman person, I don't have time to cheat and I like for my woman to be the same way. If I'm going to give my all I expect her to do the same. I rather hang out with my lady than anything. I like to go to dinner and let the person I'm with know that's it all about her. I can say that I love hard because I put my all in my relationship. it has got me in trouble a lot of times but that's just me. Mostly I want a woman that will respect me for who I am. I have seen relationships start off with love and end up going bad about money. People let money come between them and if she loves money more than me I don't want to be with her. You may have up and downs in a relationship as a man you suppose to take care of your family and I truly believe in that. When you go through the bad times I want a woman that's going to be there, sometimes a man need a shoulder to cry on too. To be able to talk to his woman about the problems he is having some people think that is soft but I think that shows maturity and communication in a relationship.

I'm just old school I guess I'm just simple I just keep it real either take me as I am or just let me go. Well that's all about me you know the rest by the letters I'll be sending. Really I just want to find a woman that loves me and will stand by me through it all. I like what you said about loving the mind first, I feel the same way then when you start making love it will be so much better. When I think about us the song just a couple of forever's come to my heart for us.

Rainiee: To Trojan well I'm going through a rough patch and now we need to know how we looking at this friendship to grow into more or is it just a friendship. I haven't had my vehicle and it has been tough riding the city bus. I really can't depend on people. Folks will show their true colors when you need them for something. It's just hard when you gave your all to others. I will give my last just to get the door lamed in my face. Finally to top it all off the toilet flooded in the hall and bedroom.

It is not gone to be no free test driving on this lot, no free cookies, no extra gravy, no spare tires, no free milk without buying the cow first, no three-some, no 70/30, 60/40 it's 50/50 or 100/100 or it will not be me and you up in here. I don't share nacho's yo's or m&m and the cleanup lady not welcome at my house, I like my m&m with my own nuts thank you.

CHAPTER THREE

Trojan: Hey Boo How are you doing, are you having a good day? I know you said you was having a rough day because of the flooding, don't let that get to you it's just the way the devil try to ease in and take over. Then the next thing you will be arguing with the kids and yourself. You are on my mind all the time and being able to find a job and do the things I want to do. I be thinking am I foolish or have I found my queen, I have already pictured us on a date how it will go what will go wrong. I just better take it one day at a time, you know like what you want in a man, am I the man you are looking for? All this go through my mind. Can I make you happy in the bedroom all that comes to mind? Do you know like what you looking for sexually or you looking for love? I know both go together but I rather have the love but don't get me wrong I love sex just as much as the next man.

You might be one of them freaky women ☺ and I might not be able to handle you☺. The more I read about you the more I have feelings for you. **It's almost like we are looking for the same thing just to serve God, and be happy.** Because you said something like people test driving before going on was you talking about to see if I'm good in bed? Woman you are a trip ☺ I don't need to test drive because if I keep test driving I will never end up with the right one.

I was in a relationship that cost me a lot and to say I lost and wasn't in love with her neither. That's why I'm taking my time and getting to know a person first I rather be alone than to go through the motions of just having lust for someone. Hell I'm getting too old for that. From the first day I saw you at my sister house I had a crush on you and *just let you get away then but not now I'm I coming for you Boo. We are going to see if it's meant to be till next time you are in my heart Boo.* Can I get a couple of forevers, love that song.

Rainiee: By this time we are talking into seeing if we going to be a couple and his letters are *going both ways about God, then he hits on sex then he backs it up with I'm just saying what comes across my mind about how I'm feeling about you.* Then I write a letter on how you doing and so many Bible verses. Ok now he playing with me keep slipping sex in, I'm fin to put him in there so I find this saying where it seems so dirty then it's not. You need to learn a person mindset first make love to the mind before you make love to their body.

Trojan: I would like to say that I'm sorry that I have not wrote my days have been hectic I have been working long shifts and I be tired when I get in but know this that you have been on my mind and in my heart every day. I'm sounding so caught up like we are in love or something or we been doing this a long time. But know that I do have feelings for you very much I don't know how you feel but I want to keep this going. To hear from you, *you got me hooked on you now you have gave me a little taste(not sex just talking and writing) and I just got to have more.* I had a dream about you we was a family, it was crazy because I was saying where this coming from is?

I just enjoy you I just want you in more ways than one. I want to give you the moon and stars your heart desire. I want to be that man that makes you smile and try to make your dreams come true. I want to be the first and the last in your life because the rest of them were nothing but busters in the way for a real man to come along and bring joy to your heart and in your life. I'm not gone to front you will be the first and last woman I'll see. I will pursue you that's my mission right now until you get tired of me.

I don't know if I have a chance with you, I don't know you have not told me if you want to try to make something **and turn it into a dream.**

Poem

When I think about you I smile

When I think about you it reminds me of a nice spring day with the flowers blooming in a valley

When I think about you my heart just flutters

When I think about you I think about us walking down the beach holding hands and madly in love

You are always in my heart Boo, just a couple of forever.

CHAPTER FOUR

Rainiee: How you doing my Trojan? I just need a clear understanding about when you say you looking for your queen, because you saying one without the other. You want a queen or a wife that's a queen? How do you plan to live? Are you planning to live life as a worldly man or a man of God in this world? So I need to know I'm not here to play any games or mind rhymes, I'm forty and you about to be forty-six, we both have lived a wild life at some point. God kept me from getting any STD's from the whores I was faithful to Amen! So I have to be very clear and upfront when I ask a guy what are you looking for or want right now? I'm not a booty call, get your nut off or an after eleven pm call only, my hotel getting more tail days are over. If you're not my lifetime partner stop wasting my time.

The only games I want to play are role-playing with me forever, to get hurt is heartbreaking so I don't want to give my all out to swain anymore. I want a love like never before that will make up for the lost time and I know that one day the Lord will call our number and I pray to God it won't be so hard. I'm trying to see if you are that man that will be my bond, seeing where you stand at in your walk with God first then us. I'm not trying to move out of place I need to know if it's God's will for you and me to be a couple forever KEEP IT 1000 ALWAYS. I have learned how to wait and not rush because if you rush without reading the fine print it's gone blow up in your face.

If at times I don't seem mushy it's just I have a wall up to my feeling's and before I open them I need to know this is real and won't break me. I want a fill up that won't run dry at all; I'm just waiting to see what will become of this also. Yes I ask what's on your mind and how you feeling I want to feel what you are feeling, I'm not trying to be controlling, I just want to share with you your thoughts, visions and everything. If we are to have each other from head to toes back to back. Words can mean so much more when applied people have taken away the meaning of words; "I love you" mean they just want sex from you. I can't stand to hear when they disrespect you because you don't give yourself up calling you a (whore- Thot the new meaning in the streets) or a Bi***.

I will ask you things not to be preaching to you or anything just trying to stay in line of the will of God. Thanks for asking about my little issue and my kids. Glad to see we're not grandparents yet. I see your daughter is grown up how times fly's. Just doing my best to keep my works right in all I do. I heard the song forever's you told about wow real touching.

There's something I think that you should know, It's not that I shouldn't really love you, Let's just take it slow we can talk it over, I need to know before we make promises to each other that what morals we stand on. Because when I think of you it makes me smile so happy. Just want to be sure-footed. Got to know who you loving and falling in love with, Got to keep the fire burning and the love turning and rolling (Janet Jackson). Got to know that I'm the only extra gravy, spare tire, the sugar that makes your tea or coffee, the only sprinkles on your ice cream with a cherry on top, the pork for your chops, the beef on your buns. When we get to know each other and we're both feeling each other stronger.

I'm tired of fast moves, I've got a slow groove, On my mind, I want a man with a slow hand, I want a lover with an easy touch I want somebody who will spend some time, Not come and go in a heated rush, I want somebody who will understand when it comes to love(Pointer Sisters).

I want something real I need a Love that will be there for you. Ain't anything like the real thing, don't let me be lonely. Fire and Desire these are some songs that come to mind when I think of you there's more I don't want to over explode before my time. Are you my roller coaster, my double barrel, my electric drive, my sho enough, my note when the music stops, my still?

Trojan: Here it is Sunday I'm thinking of you right now listening to church music and writing you. I feel you when you said we have to put God first because without him we are nothing, with him all things are possible. You ask me why I like you so much don't sell yourself short I'm just a lucky man that sees all the good things in you. **See the others don't see what I see and I'm glad because that gives me the chance to have you all to myself. Like I said I want to be the first and the last in your life God knows I want this to work out between us. I want a wife not a girlfriend you are beautiful and I enjoy your mind the more I listen to you the**

more I want you; you are what I have been looking for in a woman. I thank God that we meet again when I seen you my mind went blank I was like she has been around me all this time and I didn't even know it.

You have the most beautiful red skin I have seen I just like that red body and skin we would have had some beautiful kids☺. You make me smile whenever I see you missing you now can't wait to hold you in my arms and give you that dance that you been looking for. I want you to feel safe in my arms and feel the love that you have been looking for. To know that I will always be there for you, you said about being my salt and pepper and "I feel you on all that". That's why you have my heart no one has ever said that to me, to be my Bonnie and I'm her Clyde I like that. Because no matter what I will do everything in my power to make you happy. Like Luther Vandross said if this world was mind I'll give you all that I can.

But this world is ours me and you boo with God's grace and blessings who can stop us just a couple of forever. I was thinking on a first date that we take the kids and pack a lunch and go to St. Augustine and have a picnic and enjoy the sights and then maybe we can catch a movie, naw that sound corny. You know I was thinking if me and you are going to try and make this work I have to get to know your kids that is a big part of everything but I do enjoy children as you can see already when I'm with my nieces. Do you think I need to slow down on my way of thinking about us? I wish I can see you know but I see you in my dreams and they are not all sexual but most are I wish but all things come to them that wait. I will wait on that dame, I got to get my mind off that but it's hard you got me I will admit it. You already trying to be bossy I like a strong woman that knows what she wants and I hope that is me.

Just like you said I don't want this ride to end I want it to ride forever I will never lie to you or hurt you if it comes to that we should not be together I will always keep it 100,000,000. That's how much I'm committed to you and making things work there no reason to look any further because you have found the one you have been looking for and I have too you are on my heart Boo until my lips can touch yours just a couple of forever's. Love you and *don't be going a straying on me now all my love is waiting on you.*

CHAPTER FIVE

Rainiee: To my Mr. T how you doing today my Boo? I'm at or should I say I'm thinking to hard sometimes you want to know something then again you don't because you not sure how it will make others feel will it help or hurt them? Direction is better than speed many are going nowhere fast. God has a plan for your life the enemy has a plan for you, are you wise enough to know which one to battle and which one to embrace (Godfruits.com). Don't regret knowing the people that comes and goes out of your life.

Roses are red, Nuts are brown, Skirts go up, Pants go down, Body to body Skin to skin, When it's stiff you stick it in, It goes in dry and comes out wet the longer it's in the stronger it gets It comes out dripping and starts to sag....it's not what you thinking it's just a tea bag☺(poem). Yes got you on that one so keep your mind out of the gutter you won't be mad you didn't get a wet Willie, glad you liked the pictures besides the hair pulling of my hair I hear you Mr. Lover man.

 Why would turning forty-six be so hard for you? Just be patient and believe what God has and will do what he will do. We have good days and bad days we may not have everything we want but we have what we need. We may wake up with aches and pain but he bless us to wake up, our life may not be perfect but we are blessed. Yes **LORD** help me to always keep in mind that I'm your willing vessel. Pray for God to help you to always hear his call and pray in power the way he wants you to. You can't make people like, love, understand, validate, accept or be nice to you nor can you control them. It doesn't matter at the end of the day be at peace with yourself you did what you could to give your best and your intentions are well and have a pure heart pray for the best in people to see Gods hand. We have to pray for them regardless what they think of us. Always give God first and most in Jesus Christ name Amen.

Trojan: Hey Boo how are you doing I hope your day is going very well just as mines have been going. You made some key points in your letter I must be not getting my point across to you of my intentions I'm not a man who goes out and say things that I don't mean, **_I'm a man of my word and I stand by what I say I will never treat you as a whore that's is not my intention_** to try and lure you in bed and leave I can do that with any woman, everything's comes full circle and I'm not trying to break that circle. Just because I say things that are on my mind does not mean I want to jump in bed with you that takes time, I intend to take this relationship slow and let it take its course.

I have never spoke this way to another person before letting what's in my heart out no one but you know how I feel about my deep thoughts. <u>I would never sell you a dream that is not me. I would rather let you go than to break the friendship that we have. I want to take our friendship beyond and above the stars this is not a game that I'm playing why would I do that just</u> to get a piece of A**. That comes at me all the time I want one woman, one love that's just for me do you feel me? If I have said anything that has offended you it was not my intention to do so. I play at the park not with people or someone I care about you are slowly pulling down walls that I have been put up because of so much pain. I would rather be alone than to go through hurt and denial again I just want to be happy and the person that I'm with is happy too. **If its Gods will it will happen but I'm not going to rush it. Have a lot of things I need to get right in my life first.** I'm not looking for a drive-by I'm looking for the long ride and if you are that person I hope it will be to death do us part.

"Yes" that's what I said I want a queen a wife a friend a lover all in one. I have played my games I'm done with that in my life do you feel me boo. That devil always trying to slip in and mess things up I bind that devil in the name of Jesus. It's all about you Boo, you are on my mind when I go to sleep and when I wake up so let it be clear I'm committed to you and only you and it's not just for sex I respect your mind and body and your faith. What more can I say for a man that is falling for you I know we have to take it slow and I'm willing to do that. Are you seeing someone else or something I can handle it I'm a big boy? If we are going to make this work we have to be true to me and yourself because I'm coming for you boo until you tell me different. Are you having second thoughts about us please tell me now?

Rainiee: Yes it's always good to be happy and full of laughs well you have to stop trying to test drive the v-six before you learn its ins and outs through the good and bad times on fair days rainy or sun shining days. How God gone give you a diamond if you won't let go of the cubic zirconia? You have to be trained on how to hold down the position to be anchored for the storm how God gone give you his best prize if you don't know how to treat and care for his daughter until he is ready to have her back. If you not ready to maintain God house you won't get it how you want a king position and you don't know how to be a king for a queen.

At the end of the day we can't be treating God like he owe us something calling on him only when we in trouble. We have to want change in order to change for the better and give it to God to be our guide in this life. We are thy brother's keeper to help each other up when one fall to give encouraging words. To seek the presence of God's grace he gives us a choice for which side we gone to be on. So I say not only let these words come out your mouth but let them be inside your heart, mind, soul and stay strong my black king. Why let your pasts determine your future in Jesus name claim his victory don't just talk about it be about it in Jesus Christ name A' men.

Trojan: Hey Boo how you doing hope you in good health and God's grace and your kids doing well? Well I feel that you can read me like a book, I just believe if a man is able to work he should I believe in family and I believe if a man commit his self to a woman with all his heart he should take care of that woman, if I have to take a job that I don't want I will because of the dedication I have to my Boo and family. I just can't sit around and do nothing it's just a good feeling to bring home that paycheck to your woman, showing her how much you love and how committed you are to her to me that's a good feeling. One thing about me I don't mind giving up my money if everything is alright at home, that's where it starts with me if I can't come home to what I want why be there you feel me especially good loving and good meals after work.

What more can I ask for in a woman if I ask for more I think I will be greedy so you are perfect just the way you are "that's right I'm putting my claim on you right now". I just can't keep you off my mind time has seem to slowed down I can't wait to see you and be around you making you laugh and happy to show you that love can be found if you let it happen. You know I been feeling you for a very long time before this, just was too scared that I was not good enough for you and I was going through some things and then you got married, I think I was kind of mad when I found out true stuff but had moved on. Why do you think every time you came over I always mess with you that was the only way I could get your attention pretty lame aye, *I have grown up now and know how to do better. I want to be your knight and shining armor to be there to fight your battles* with you winning or losing but I always win☺.

It's just something about you Boo it always have been got me stuck. got me hooked got me falling head over heels for you got me thinking about you all the time, it's me and you against the world Boo. And with God's help we gone conquer it together just me and you. By the way you have better handwriting than me I just write slowly and you write fast I can tell, I hope you are not fast in the bedroom. You are my day and night you are and I love you for you I'm just feeling you like no other you have my mind my heart my body and soul I give it freely to you and only you with all my love Boo.

I changed a few words in your poem

Roses are red Violets are blue

Do I really have a crush on you yes and yes?

Merry (Rainiee & Trojan) goes round and round I'll never lie, cheat, steal or kill on you. Red Rover Red Rover you will never have to send me over, when you are real I'll come to stay forever Boo! Duck goose don't play me loose never that Boo, If to love you is wrong I need to know because it won't be right this love is not wrong, Snap crackle and pop you can always trust me, Dance dance don't take my prance we gone dance forever Boo.

Don't take my joy away la la la, to say the time you have already stole my joy because I give it to you freely and I will never take your joy if I do you can have all of mind. As always I love you boo always watching the stars and the moon just a couple of "forever". I was wondering will you think about marrying me and if you say yes you would have to plan it because I never been married go and look for some rings also.

Rainiee: Hello Mr. T how are you feeling and doing? Checking to see where your head is at today (laugh out loud) which one that is nasty of me it just jumped out at me. As I was saying now I'm answering your question head on laugh out loud get it ok back to the keys how do you rate what you call lovers? That is true how can you love someone if you can't love yourself? Do you love yourself now? Do you know if you hear from God? We have to just be careful of the people and not let their actions become ours. The void we feel is for God to fill and when we let him in then we become complete we are not meant to fit in with the world. Hanging in the wrong area can cause you to fall to your death or make you feel down and that is not good at all. We just have to give it to God and trust him the pain we feeling now can't compare to what joy he have coming for us. Call it out I am healed I'm delivered I'm redeemed by the Almighty God I hope this helps you out and know who and what your power source is.

My God we need your touch right now for your Holy Power to rain on us. Now to my Mr. T I pray your day has changed for you from sad to smiles and joy. I know it's gone be days that gone make you stop and say what the world is going on? Yes the enemy wants you to fail that's his problem and not mines make sure you are standing upright and doing what please God not man. I need to stop catching hell and run hell straight up outta here. When we do what the Lord says in his will then he will supply our needs we have to live for Christ and not ourselves or people. We can't let the past stop us or the enemy so you can't be feeling all broke and down because God mends all, he is the healer the savior and he can do all things for those that believe and trust him. Love you Boo and be who he called you to be a strong black man with all power in him you are my man of God.

CHAPTER SIX

Trojan: Hey boo I hope you are enjoying your day and I woke up with you on my mind while getting ready for work. Like I said it's me and you what we have only God can take it from us. The past is the past and that's where I leave it it's all about the future and us baby. I will not let anyone get in the way of our happiness; you make me feel like a man, I never met a woman that gives so much encouragement you make me feel like I can do anything. **That's one of the reasons why "I love you" yeah I said "love" just feeling you boo. You know I know I ain't the greatest man in the world but I know how to treat a woman especial the one I love.**

<u>I</u> want to be that man that shows you the things that you have never seen or done, I want to be the man that makes all your dreams come true. I want you to be the woman that makes me feel like nothing is impossible for me to do. Well you already make me feel that way anyway. My thoughts are to love and hold you and take care of you with all my heart and strength, to be the sugar in your coffee. I like that you are standing by me, I take that back "I love that" especially about the open arms waiting on me I can't wait to hold you in my arms just want to kiss them beautiful lips of yours☺. I bet you is a good kisser too, I think I do ok also never had any complaints yet. As for you cooking for me by the way that's so sweet of you thinking about me see that what makes me love you because you thinking about me smiling faces everywhere. Let me get my mind back on track☺ far as the

food I would love to have some collard greens with smoked pigtails, cornbread, fried chicken and some ice tea with lemon and for desert I would like to have a kiss from my boo a long one☺ with some ice cream. Ain't had no love in a long time not the love in the bedroom but the love of a woman that will be there for me to me that means a lot.

Loyalty is so important to me I have been betrayed so many times I mean it hurts sometimes to even think about it I try not to but leave in it the past. So I'm your T-man Hu! I'm glad to hear that because I already claim you and some of that red robin (X-rated)☺ boo! I got to get my mind out the gutter but every time I think about you I sometimes drift that way, *now just because I think about it does not mean I want it right now. Baby because remember what I said I respect your mind, body and faith but there is nothing wrong with a little foreplay hugging and kissing and don't forget touching just waiting for when we can spend time with each other. To know your ways and wants that spot that makes you crazy ☺ you know the only way to find out is we got to explore. I'm claiming the future for us baby you my ride or die chick it's all about you boo!, well boo I'm going* to end this letter but not my love for you just a couple of forever's and a lifetime, you and only you, you are in my heart boo. And like you said God first in Jesus name, Amen.   **Love you**

Rainiee: I'm sending him words from the Bible and encouraging him as a man to be a man of God that seeks God face and direction for your life. Your part is to trust God no matter what happens, he will never fail you, all ways out Him first in your life, believe in the power of prayer, stay away from drama and forgive people don't go back to your past look forward and most important don't lose faith God didn't say it would be easy but it will be worth it. More of God words because now he keep letting me know he having sex dreams and I'm letting him know that it's demonic to have those dreams. We are planning on what date we're to go on and now we expressing our feelings more about each other. I let him know that I have gave myself to God 100% I have sold out to Jesus for real and I'm not having sex until I get married so you better know that you know Jesus real good to send you what you ask for in a spouse to the "T". And to know what we want in a marriage and the bedroom because it won't be **NO TEST DRIVING UP IN HERE BEFORE WE SAY I DO. [For the readers]** And I'm trying to keep my thoughts from being dirty and nasty because this brother right here can write where you can almost see what he talking about right in front of you. And I ask him did he ask God is I'm the wife for him and I had to do the same by asking God is he the one for me before I let my feelings get deep in this brother. Now that you asked me to marry you and plan a wedding.

Now he talking about foreplay is ok when can you have foreplay that don't lead into sex that's the reason for it what he made of if he can play in the fire and not get burned, the only guys I heard of being able to it was Shadrach, Meshach, and Abednego with the Son of GOD there with them (Daniel 3).

Trojan: As I look on life this world has become so evil I believe the gift that God gave me was I can discern people I use to think I was crazy to see what God shows you about a person. I was wrong for using it for my advantage. I don't play when it comes to children I don't like to see them being taken advantage of you have to get to the root of the problem to help not just treat people wrong I don't like that at all. He gives all of us gifts we just have to tap into them. I have to thank God for keeping me alive from all that test driving I did and was doing taking chances with my life I can't even count how many times the Lord has blessed me thank you Lord.

I just got to stay focus that's why I say to you be slow with me for it may take time but no matter what I will be there for you as a friend, your lover if you want it to be or your husband if it Gods will he only knows the future we can only give him praise and fear him daily. I write these words to you because this how I feel for you I don't write them just to write them you are in my heart where you have always been rather you accept them or not it will not change.

I sometimes wonder what you see in me I just want to be loved and not die and leave this world without someone loving me is a fear I cannot shake, to die alone with nobody there or to care for you. This is just how I feel I just look for the good in people. I use to teach Bible study somehow I let go. Then I ask you do you want a guy like me a man with so many dreams that have not come to pass, A guy with so much passion that he keep it bottle up inside because he don't want to get hurt. It's me I guess you probably may think I'm nuts.

But for real though I'm just a good guy that people don't see but when it comes to you it seems that I can show you the real me. The real Trojan Lowes not the one they be talking about all the time just my view how I feel.

You is something else woman talking about a monkey wrench what's the size of a monkey wrench anyway you got me thinking about that driving me up the wall, I am going to be able to please you I know a woman love to have good sex and they look for monkey wrench what do you want a man or a porn star I just work with what God gave me. I do try to please both ways I just hope it's enough to please you baby I have not had no problems before on what I do. Some woman are hard to please and some are not some want a porn star and be tow all up that's not good, I want something light and sweet like cotton candy☺.

Rainiee: We all are at an age to understand what's going on in this world and in the mist of me reading from Trojans letter I asked questions about things some was being funny because of what he wrote to me. To be clear we did not have letter sex and I did not engage back to lead him to think it was go to happen before I get married. You do have to be careful on what you talk about and let someone speak into your ear gates, it may seem innocent I say just be careful because if you are not married and saved it should not be a part of an everyday conversation piece unless it's an open group topic for learning how to be Godly women and men of God. The enemy is very slick and wants to take you out anyway necessary. I feel God is calling me out to become more involved in ministry and my Pastor licensing me as Minister in this October twenty-fourteen so I need to be clear on my walk in God and my feelings about us. I can't say I serve God and sin all day and stepping up to be an example of who I serve. How about when you come I fix you dinner and what would you like to have prepared for you.

Trojan: Good Morning seeing that it's early and you are on my mind and in my heart first I'm happy about you becoming a Minister very happy for you. Well let me introduce myself to you my name is Trojan Lowes I'm 5'11 and 195 pounds I have light brown eyes my favorite color is blue I enjoy sunset's walks, sports and I was born the six of March and will be turning forty-six this year two-thousand and fourteen. Let me say that love come in many forms when I say I love you it means that I love your smile I love the way you write letters I love your bossiness' I love the way you care for people I love your style. I know that love have to come in time with two people when you say do I want you to be the one yes I do. I understand that you have become a Minister and that's great and you have to carry a higher standard than most folks and I respect that, **but I'm who I am a man that's changing every day if you are asking me about my faith I love God just like the next person.**

Do I live his way like I suppose to no I don't I want to one day become one of God's soldiers yes but that will not happen overnight it's a process see you got to go back to the potter's wheel to get reshaped and remolded. And I feel that's what I'm on now the potter's wheel I just take it day by day whatever his will it will be done and all I can do is pray about it and ask for his grace, mercy and love. Do you want me to go to church with you? I have no problem with that I read my Bible every day I do in my own way and let God do the rest. ***I will not rush into something that I have not thought through, I don't just do things I think it through first and then give it to God.*** If it work out it's his will if not it wasn't meant.

So my commitment to you is real to change to life. Baby I say if you are feeling me which I hope you are I say let's go with it and see what happens, it was a reason you wrote me. Out of all people you was the one nothing is done for nothing I believe that what we do in life is meant to happen I just don't believe in why this happened junk. You can't stop Gods will I have tried and it just doesn't work so I go with his way. What more can I say more about you and me I know how I feel about you and that's not gone change the more I talk to you the more I feel you. I have my shortcomings don't we all I tell you these things because I have nothing to hide. I'm not ashamed of my past because they have been washed away God says so.

Rainiee: Yes my T bear you have to keep your head up and believe what God word says and seek him every day to see what he want you to do. Got to be strong for yourself plus you have a daughter that needs you long as you got God first and the head of your life you can't lose. I send my warmest open arms to you and my love for you. **We must pay attention to what someone is saying to you listen or read close the red flags are there you got to watch and listen for them and if you don't know it's best to always seek God for the truth can't go wrong if it's his will for you. In** the mist of all I need to know if this God will for me and Trojan to be together and God will answer you if you want the truth from him. Many of us don't want the truth because it's not what we want and there's nothing wrong with giving someone Gods word it's up to them to use it. They say game recognize game just be careful. How you say you love me and now you explain it in a different format? I know you can love someone and you can be in love with someone or just care for a person and what you want isn't always good for you. Everything that glitter ain't gold and everything that is sweet isn't good for you have you ever heard this saying before? Just be careful not to be anyone fool, play mat, booty call, after twelve midnight, SpongeBob, sucker, dum-dum stick, my right now but not the right one or just wait for nothing wasting your life away.

I was told long time ago why would he buy the cow when he getting the milk for free and it toke me some years to get it but I still didn't get it because I thought if I flipped it on the guy I was on top. No I was just cheating myself out from the truth and after having three children I get it and learning how to pray for change and what I need.

Trojan: Good morning Ms. Rainiee boo I see you think you are a backup you was never that or will never be one and my past were the test drives you are my Mercedes-Benzes. I had a hectic week at work getting all cut up I like to keep my skin clean and my temper being tested these co-workers just thought they was gone have me do all the work while they play around got to stay away from that area let them push me to get mad, can't teach anger management if you blow up. For a second I misunderstood and thought you gave up on us ok but you are a queen and I will treat you like one and I will always respect and treat you like a woman is supposed to be treated. To take care of you if it's in my power I look at you as a woman of God and a person who truly cares about life and everything around her that is why I truly love being in your presents your joy is contagious you give me uplifting words. Not only to me but others as well so keep being Rainiee boo baby and great things are going to come to you and keep being my boo forever and ever and let me have some red robin:). He writes a poem for me and as I get ready to end this letter if you do not know most beautiful woman you are in my heart and on my mind may God bless you 1,000,000,000 times over until I get to see your beautiful smile.

Rainiee: To my strong black man of God how are you feeling today? Hoping you is no longer feeling down or sad. And by the way I don't want no porn star just a man that can do what it takes and I don't know the size of a monkey wrench, I go by the condom size lifestyle, magnums lol (laugh out loud) which you can tell me which one you fit (lol) just tripping. But keeping it real on all levels 6, 7, 8, 9, and 10, 11 inches (lol) to be real I use to know the size I have forgot it's been a long time for me. So anyway getting back to the subject just keep smiling my boo!! I'll have your back and side front too :) keep it real and right XOXOXOXOXOXOXOOXOXOXOXOOXOXOXXO's miss you much time will mend you together. Now we draw hearts with our name in them. We just got to trust in the Almighty God and do as he says in this life and walk, do we yield to do his will and serve him with our all. No matter what we go through our problem is not bigger than our God, do you believe that we can't worry about it just got to pray about it. So I send you my love and warmest open arms to keep you.

Trojan: How are you doing boo I hope the sky is so blue and you are in the best health? I have my boo and our good conversations I really like the way you give me the truth I really do. I do have to say you are bossy already trying to boss me around just always thinking boo but anyway vibing about us.

Feelings-was so happy by the words you put in your letter now you claiming me now Hu! ☺ **I love that** the way you talk about how you got my back and everything and your trust in me with your heart I promise I will try not to break it because I have already given mines to you with two happy hearts how can we go wrong ☺.

Thoughts-wanting to take you places you never been before to height's beyond pleasures to be that man that will always be there for you no matter what we go through I want to grow old with you if it's Gods will. Do you like flowers and what kind? "Dame" lost focus for a second sorry☺.

You know I like to play a lot of sports do you like to go to the park we can play someone on one ball or one on one now that would be a good game Dame lost focus again☺. But I like to walk keeps the body fit I'm in pretty good shape to be almost forty-six playing ball a lot and walking we should keep that up. In this life there are many choices and we just have to know its God plans for us to prosper some will accept it's from God and some won't. You just have to come to point about what way you gone to go in life at the crossroad fork the blood have already been spilled. Love you be safe just a couple of forever's.

Rainiee: As we go on he's hitting good points about life and his feelings for me and there are parts that I didn't put in this book because I'm here to make valuable points on life not make a porn novel. My purpose is to be a help to the lost we have enough porn in this lifetime and to let you at the end of this book what happens for us. Tell me some things you like doing and want to do soon. Trojan told me something's that he asks to keep between him and I so I didn't write about it you can't kiss and tell everything.

Trojan: Today ha! Well just checking in on my boo to see how you are doing I hope you are doing well. We only can get what he gives us just a reminder we all go through things just know I hear you and I'm feeling you far as your feelings and thoughts, what they are. A man can be many forms I have seen and read and it takes a man to choose that perfect woman she may not be perfect to others, but to the one that loves her, and he will always say that she's the perfect one for him. Well to let you know I like reading books also a good way to retain information on the brain. Now these Jags losing to Miami but my team are the Dallas Cowboys and we doing well. I took your advice about talking to my sister so we can be on better terms, already being bossy ain't you, I'm glad to hear that you got my front and back what you saying boo :) but you are the one that makes me think because of the words you say. I know you have been through something's but it does not matter to me I see you as my friend and much more. But boo I send you the best of everything that I can give you and that's my friend, my love, respect and my heart just a couple of forever's forever's! Trojan&Rainiee.

Hey boo how are you doing I hope and pray that you are healthy and safe. I had a headache so bad yesterday that stop me from talking to you now I'm better than I heard from you, Now about this bossy stuff baby I have learned that someone out of the relationship has to be bossy but when you have two people that is bossy oh boy. But being bossy in different situations is ok sometimes you have to put your foot down. So baby keep being bossy I love that be bossy in the bedroom too now☺. Always thinking about us you ever been so nervous about something I feel it's like I have been waiting for so long and you have finally found it just happy faces baby.

I have been waiting for a young lady like you for a long time, the thing is that sometimes it is right in your face and you don't realize it until you sit down and find out about someone like love and being loved to have someone that will always be there for you through the bad and good days to come. To me as a man there is no better feeling than to have the love of a woman and to know no matter what we got each other backs. I be sitting looking at your pictures and I be saying how did I get so lucky to find a beautiful woman like this I be like dame whoever had you before me must did not listen to you or something how can I put this it's like I hear your wants in your words I feel the pain and happiness and your passion about things. It's like your words affect me to in such a way I don't know maybe I'm thinking too much baby you know me always thinking. I just want you to have the greatest date ever like nothing you ever had nothing but the best for you baby!

But I know that we have something special I just know it don't tell me how I know I just feel it just like I feel you boo! I wish for you to be blessed. Trojan Lowes & Rainiee Lowes

Rainiee: Just like I said the brother is on point with his lines and words he speak and if you just starting in a relationship and have not been taught what to look for you will be in trouble. Not that I'm trying to give away the dirty talk he was saying to me I will say if I wasn't save this book might catch on fire, Trojan words on how he wanted me had me needing a cold shower on days thank God I am a strong woman that prays hard to Jesus and can wait. Don't get me wrong Trojan has a good heart and is educated that will plcase a woman in all ways.

That's why we need to teach our kids how to be dated before they go buck wild and the world teach them, which is dangerous grounds if they think they looking for love or to be loved and the person turns out to be a wolf or an abusive person. We have these monsters out here pimping the children out turning them out to crack heads, we must rise above underground mentality and help save the people.

If I wasn't rooted in Jesus I may have failed to having a unmarried relationship all over again, that's why it is important to know that if you are living for God Jesus we can't do the thing we use to we just can't. We have to change our circle on who we hang with, what we say or talk about the words that come out of our mouths. In common sense the same way that you would not want a doctor working on you that don't know what they doing or a hamburger maker building you a house and they don't have any training on how to lay a foundation for a house.

Trojan: Good morning boo it seems like you are happy I hope I'm a big part of that happiness because since the first day I receive that letter from you I have been having smiling faces all the time☺ ☺ . My mind has been all over the place always thinking about you it's like you have invaded my mind ☺ I tell you one thing that has never happen before but I have not had that many girlfriends. They have liked me but I never perused them probably because we had nothing in common they see thug and like that about me but that was not who I was and when they realize it they lose interest. But anyway I'm glad because if I was still with them I would have missed you and that's not happening giving you up no! I refuse to let that devil get in the way of our happiness yes I said our, I'm putting my foot down on

LIPS OF FIRE

that☺.

It's amazing how a person can go from not really looking for someone to just falling head over heels but I guess you got that good stuff☺ or maybe it's that redskin of yours☺ but I know what it' is you are very upfront about everything you know what you want and you go get it I'm the same way. Last night I had a dream about you now don't go putting your mind in the gutter it was a good dream we was a couple and we was doing good together boy did I get some kisses from you, all in public. But anyway I rather dream about you than anyone else I will ride and I will die for mines, my answer is you boo till the end boo.

Now you can't be all nervous and stuff when you stand up there to speak at the church for your trail sermon just think about me and you will get through it. I hope it went well for you and you had them jumping out of their seats but stand tall for God for you are one of his children. I remember my first one I just got up there and went at it I wish I had notes but I didn't this is what I said before I went up there Father let the words that come out my mouth be yours and only yours not mines in Jesus name and I did it study to show thy self-approved and it will come. I see you looking good that's what I like for my woman to be dressed it makes me look good also my bad baby had slip off (X-rated thoughts) get focus it's just you look so good on these pictures I can't help myself.

Just want to hold you in my arms and whisper sweet things in your ears and the master says there is a time for everything and

it's our time now do you believe that boo? I do. When is your birthday baby you have not told me you ain't lying about your age are you? You not twenty-one are you trying to throw that young thing on me would you? ☺ It's a time for everything boo and your time will come know that our time will come. Trojan&Rainiee forever and ever.

Hey beautiful how are you doing today? Well if no one has told you how beautiful you are today I'm telling you most beautiful of all women. I enjoy our talks and conversations I just enjoy you "Lord" knows I do I can't wait to be with you not in a sexual way well that too☺ just want to spend more time with you so we can cuddle watching movies. Just want to feel the warmth from your body just want to be loved by the woman that I love just want you to show me all that you have and I show you that I just want you boo and nobody else only God can replace you from my heart.

1. I like to cook and Im pretty good at it.

2. I enjoy all kinds of food. I don't like crabs. Ihate them but I have ate them before I chose not to eat it.

3. Baby I have been a lot of places Atlanta, down south, up north.

4. I plan on taking a cruise you want to come.

5. I love to fish but I never catch anything.

6. I swim but not in the pool bad on the skin the beach yes.

7. I can't sing but I try don't play any instruments baby do you.

8. Now I like to play board games baby all kinds.

9. I like water fights and to wrestle but (X-rated) ☺ sorry baby lost focus only when it comes to you I lose focus.

I went to the doctor and got my tests back and my HIV test clean bill of health. And thank you again about caring for me to see that I get what I need you know I love you right that's one of the reasons you got a beautiful heart and I can't wait to share it with you baby can't wait. Well I'm not going to say much more just that you are in my heart baby let's make this last forever baby just a couple of forever's baby. Always in my heart love Trojan& Rainiee Lowes ha! (Drawing names in a heart). PS oh you like being bossy all the time Hu we gone see about that Ms.Rainiee or should I say Mrs. Lowes Hu one day baby one day I will have you all to myself with a ring on your finger if its Gods will. Always Trust In The Lord.

CHAPTER SEVEN

Rainiee: As we go on getting to find out about each other expressing how we feeling about each also but the key fact is to **know if God told you that this is your mate he has given to you as a child of God** and you not running off of yourself. I have to catch up on the letters he wrote me to know what I wrote him so just bear with me and I hope that I'm really helping you in the process. I have learned that this can go either way as well this could have been a woman letting a man know that they are meant to be together, she the pusher of it and leading him to think he is. We have to be truthful if we are a born-again creation just know how to relay the word we give to others sometimes we still gone offend people without knowing it.

Well I walked to the store and came back home and was getting ready to leave out for work and dropped my bus pass so now am running down (in dress shoes) the sidewalk checking for the bus pass so I don't miss the bus. I found it yes now my feet hurt this is just too much I have to leave and two-hours before so I don't be late to work I need my car fixed. How do you rate love? You asked me do I like flowers yes I do roses are great now I enjoy the beauty of carnations they last longer to me.

Trojan: How are you doing baby? I hope and pray that your days have been filled with joy and peace. Those are the best days sometimes I just wish for a day of total peace I take what I can get for another day to get it right. On what you said about hurting other people feel I try to be positive I rather have the truth about it saves a lot of drama I think everybody should be that way but that's not going to happen. I'm alive because of Jesus Christ thank you Lord I give him thanks a lot got to give him the praise.

You are always in my heart boo got me over here thinking about you all in my mind and junk but I thank you for the determination that I see in your letters. Plus all the other traits you have that brings out the best of you. Just got to pray baby because that devil be moving he know that you are doing everything that's right and he wants to mess it up to put him in his place boo and move on, because he can't do nothing to you unless you allow it. I have them days like nothing is going right but I pray and ask God for help then I usually make it through it. About that you around here speed walking and hurt your heel did it hurt badly boo? I wish I was there I could rub and make it feel better. Now you losing the bus pass that was too funny got to get your car fixed.

Wisdom is the reward you get for a lifetime of listening. A leader is one who knows the way and shows the way the best leader is the one who has the vision to choose good men to do what needs to be done. Just a few things that help me with life when it comes to doing things these are my quotes on life and leadership and listening. I'm a good listener you are never talking too much about yourself that's how I'm getting to know your ways bossy☺. I feel like I'm getting old turning forty-six kind of scared got a lot to get done and praying the Lord gives me time to do it like get married, travel spend time with you.

Try to make all your dreams come true for us, watch my grandkids grow up, just get life right and live for the Lord and have fun.

If you like the life you have keep doing what you're doing, if you want to change do it.

Hey beautiful I hope you are doing very well and in God's grace, you know I just feel great I got a beautiful woman that standing by me but the best part is that you are a God fearing woman and I never had that. **The more and more I talk to you through our letters I fall more and more in love with you and that's strange to meet a person and just fall for them yes baby you got me**. I mean you are always on my mind I just want to be around you and make you laugh, make you happy and just be there for you always through the good and the bad. When I think of you my heart skips a beat I get all happy and stuff I be wondering am I falling too hard am I coming on to strong will that make you step away because of that. I never felled this hard for a woman before not even my daughter mother I think I never was in love with her because she don't know the things that you know about me.

You are the only woman that I have really open up to like this being able to tell you my wants, likes, my dreams and to tell you how I feel about you, you know me better than my own family, I be thinking how is that and it scares me sometimes because you got me hooked. I just want to spoil you like you never before if I have to work two jobs to keep my baby spoiled ☺ now, I'm just saying if you with me I will always try to treat you as the queen you are as a man. All men are looking for their queen, is it not right for asking to spoil his queen but I think it go beyond that who knows what God is going to do? I can't wait to I get out so we can be together.

The days are short and the nights are long by day I think of her when I woke but the day is still short oh how I wish the days was longer just giving me the chance not to go to these lonely nights for its these times that I think of you the most for these times you invade my mind my heart my bones and I say why do I have to go through so much pain? But then I came to realize that one day me and my baby gone be together soon so come on lonely nights and short days (thoughts of Trojan☺). (Poem)

You said something about telling and not keeping anything from one another I agree with that 100% that's important just got to keep it real I'm not going to lie, I rather for us not to be together before I lie to you. Baby I will always be 100% to you if not more I don't like to share and I will protect mines to especially at night in the bedroom I will be the police there to protect you☺. Baby I'm looking for the same thing a love that will stay forever and ever always thinking baby. You are worth more than money baby worth more to me than anything that I can have for what it is worth any way I rather have you as always you are very beautiful and in my heart. Love you boo Trojan& Rainiee forever and ever in Jesus name A' men   Ms. Bossy& Tro

Rainiee: I was letting him know that everyone goes through it how you hold on and react in the storm is gone to be the victory are you gone stay in it to come out or give up before you even get started? **IN the time we learning about each other I'm feeding him the word of God and encouraging him to be a strong Godly black man that loves Jesus and God will give you your heart desire when you seek him first**. We just got to stand firm on his word and live according to his word. You can't let them folks in there get you mad and bent out of shape if you teaching Bible study to them saying you are a believer and to close for you to come home, just walk away and know that God has a plan for all of us to live. Take the time out and look at the little things in life then the bigger things will come plus I will take care of all your needs ☺ baby☺. We have to forgive and let go of the pain of being hurt in our relationships, family, friends and enemy's which we both have had bad relationships that cut very deep.

Trojan: **Song**-never let you go, I don't know I was feeling bad not in health wise but in my spirit that devil trying to make me think we will never make it. **Thoughts-**I'm in love feeling happy but I'm glad to have you in my life and will not let that devil spoil our happiness. I was surprised at the question you asked me, I Thought you already knew well since you don't know yes and yes and many more yes that I love you. I love everything about you I love your smile everything. I just have to wait and show you how I really feel about you Ms. Bossy you not going anywhere, where you go I go your problems are my problems, And I wouldn't feel this way if I didn't love you baby, you are in my heart and I can't get you out of it and I don't want to get you out of my heart. Why would I do that I have been waiting on you to ask me that question now do you feel the same way is I am on a one-way street. I know how you feel a little bit by your letters but you have never said it I have enough love for both of us baby.

Thoughts will God bless me with a good job for I will be able to take care of you I'm scared about that don't want to lose you over that but I will work anywhere if it pay good always thinking boo. Just want to make you happy don't want you to have to look at any other man than me, I want to be the air for you I want to be that support you need when you are down and with God how can it go wrong but I'm always thinking baby.

Thinking what if I can't do what I suppose to do will she still love me or will she give up on us I bind that devil from my mind and my life you are my queen my friend and hopefully you are going to be my lover hopefully you are the last woman I will ever make love to forever baby that's what I'm looking for and you☺ baby you must not know you got me hooked like a fish going after some bait on a line. Lord Jesus bless me and this relationship with Rainiee and Trojan Lowes for without you and your grace how can it work, I just want to be loved by you baby just you. There's no one else and there was not no one before you came just pretenders trying to find out something about what I'm going to do but you broke down all the walls and made it to my heart, where you have stayed and I want you to stay forever and ever baby I do love you. But I'm going to take what God gives me and not complain when I don't have it.

I mean the only time I really lose control is when I have these thoughts of you and I say dame I can't be there to tell her, I have to remember and put it on paper. Missing you baby missing you missing what I know is to come missing love missing you and only you missing the cuddle time we could be having missing that smile that is on your face missing being face to face with you just missing you.

Love, love, love where art thy love when will love find me or has love already found me and I don't even know it, love is just not a four letter word it's what everybody wants and that is love. I want a love so strong that nothing can break it but God for love is just not sex it's having a love for one another passion the way they walk just the way a person smile the things that we say to each other. Just to say I love you and when it's to the person that you truly love it will mean something to them but that's just my thinking but I know it's out there, have we found what we have been looking for a long time?

Like you said you have to go through something and lose something and then you will know where you went wrong or the person you were with went wrong. That's why I don't go around saying I love you to people because they may take it the wrong way, I only say it when I mean it don't want no one with hurt feelings. And I say this to you yes I do love you and I'm counting down the day to let our love for each other grow that's all I want baby is you to love me as I love you and I know it will take time who can measure time but God. So we might have a long time finding out☺ I'm with you to the end baby ride or die love you boo. Stay safe and in God's grace always in JESUS name Amen   Trojan& Rainiee forever   PS you ever thought about getting married again just thinking baby?

Rainiee: Is this helping you so far are you getting the scene of what's going on? This is for my readers not to Trojan. Ok I will be back let's see what else Mr. T got going on.

Trojan: Hey most beautiful woman to me and God, how are you doing baby I hope you are in the best of health and in God's grace and love.

Yesterday was a good day I got to talk to my baby had smiling faces all over the place had so much to say but when I heard your voice everything just went blank see what you do to me boo. Got me all speechless and stuff and you know I always got something to say but that day I was at a loss of words. You know this Christmas was different from the others I have spent so many alone but this time when you have someone special in your life. When I woke up I thank God and then you pop right in my mind boo. Then you know my mind went there(X-rated thoughts) and I started laughing because I said what if I was to show up to your house in a big red bow then I said you would probably call the police on my behind. Oh boy if you could show up at my door dressed like that it would be great then I woke from daydreaming wishing upon a star hoping it would come true.

Baby I just go back and reread the letters and I see things I missed the first time and letting them soak in and smiling ever where taking my time to enjoyed what you said to me. Then I say wee Lord help me with this beautiful woman of mines I truly do love you boo love the way you talk and be upfront about things love that, looks like I might need some energy drinks messing with you Hu☺. Baby don't be upset with people you know how they is so don't worry be happy hey that's a song you remember that little mommy, I don't know why I called you that little mommy it just came to my mind that's all boo. Oh so you rather dream about a cookie than me Hu you mean to tell me that I haven't invaded your dreams yet not even a little bit baby. You have invaded my dreams and to think a cookie beat me out Hu maybe I should dress up like a cookie then maybe you might have dream about me(X-rated thoughts) sorry got to focus I'm back would that help if I dressed like a cookie maybe I get a little attention in your dreams.

Dame it's like we are on the same page with things with loyalty, trustworthy, passionate and baby I am willing to fight for you. You are in my heart before I let you go they will have to do something to me because the love I have for you goes deeper than the ocean baby deeper than anything. before I let you go hey that's a song ain't it baby and you are right at the end of the day that's all I want is to be loved and respected and understood baby I feel the same way make a brother work three jobs with that kind of talk:) but that's why I love you Rainiee you are a woman that deserves all that.

Yes baby I did think you thought that's all I wanted and I don't want you to think that I just love you baby, I can do without sex just like you to just be around you is good enough for me spending time. Just laying around cuddling together watching TV or something that's just my way baby but I do love sex though but it's not why I want to be with you. I think a lot of people miss out on love because they look for people that have money or what they can do for them instead of looking for what's good about the person. You may find yourself the richest person in your life and I'm not talking about money am talking about being rich with love and happiness and health and serving God now to me that's being rich.

CHAPTER EIGHT

Trojan: As I sit and think about you and how far we have come, I wonder if this a dream or am I awake. The joy I have now I can't explain it but here comes the pain and hurt, thinking that one day you will be gone where will that leave me? It seems that someone or something always get in the way of my happiness or is it me getting in the way? By the way I wonder what Kelly doing I just laugh at that because I don't even know her like that, she don't know me like my favorite color is. I don't have anything against her she just my daughter mother; you are the only woman I'm looking for nobody can replace you. Well back to you I feel two heads are sometimes better than one, just want to see you happy no more sad faces nothing but smiling faces. That's an order I'm putting my foot down on this one :) baby.

I only have my daughter always wanted a son never had the chance a boy to carry on the name. When was the last time someone called you baby hey baby?

Rainiee: Did he just come out the blue and talking about his baby mommy? which is funny because I had a dream that some funny stuff was gone to happen. Not that I'm looking for this warning comes before destruction happens. Do I need to see if she reaching out to him so they can get back together or is this buster talking to another female? He tells me all these fairy tales better than popcorn with butter hotter than the sun, hot and spicy love. Trojan asking me if I'm ready to be Mrs. Lowes and how he is ready and he may be a little jealous and want me all to him, telling me to go pick out rings and plan the wedding to look for the dress. The light coming on telling me to paste my moves and to take one day at a time and wait for Trojan to come here.

Trojan: Hey Mrs. Lowes how are you doing you know you are most beautiful woman to me baby I'm going to marry you baby you not gone to have to wait long, just let me know how much it's gone to cost. Want everything to be right for us this will be my first wedding I don't want to half step, I love you more than anything. We will have to get a bigger place to live because the kids need their space too, can't have my girls cramped up. If you don't know by now I'm not going anywhere you are the love of my life and I love you and only you if I have not told you enough then I will tell you for the rest of our lives. Don't worry baby I'm yours and you are mines I love you Rainiee Lowes.

I just want to have a love that's gone to last forever and a woman that only loves me. Just too always be able to open up to you about everything talk about my problems, to build on trust from the start. I almost gave up on love because of the lies and heartbreaks that changed when I meet back up with you and we started talking. Just to have something to mean something that's a big difference without all the lying and games being played. I want more for myself my queen, my wife and my family because when I leave this earth I want people to say that I was a good father, husband that took care of his family while serving God.

What more can a man ask for money yes while I'm here but I can't take it with me. Li-Ma we are on point with our thoughts we just want the same thing in life, I have been waiting for a long time for you to come into my life. (X-rated thoughts) I love you woman I really do no bull crap, to fall deeply in love Trojan& Rainiee Lowes our day is finally Li-Ma plan baby plan if I don't like it baby I will let you know. Always in my heart and in my mind baby, love you Rainiee Lowes with all my heart never leave me baby because I will never leave you Trojan. To say today that I'm in love with a woman that makes me smile, makes me mad and have my heart in her hands to do as she please a woman that I have completely given myself to and I have not done this before.

I give it to you freely because of the love I have for you, a heart that has been broken but now it's fixed because of you Li-Ma so it's yours boo do you want this heart to be all yours do you want this man's love forever and ever? Do you want to lay in my arms and tell me how much you love me like I want to do, do you want to make love to me all night and have me calling out your name do you baby? Do you want to make this last forever I do baby? I want to spend the rest of my life with you do you want me forever baby? Love you love you wedding bells baby wedding bells but you will have to plan it baby and I will do my part we are a team baby we are one, what's mines is yours baby always.

See now you will have to listen to your husband and don't make me have to put my foot down ☺ or will I have to go through the rest of our lives you not listen to me baby ☺ I still will love you. Everything will be alright for us as long as we put it in Gods hand and baby I already see you as my wife we just have to make it official, so don't be scaring me like you have changed your mind. My mind is made up you are mines!! ☺ I got your back and your front too ☺ (X-rated thoughts) hey Lil-Ma can you stand the rain I know I can baby. The rain the snow and whatever else is gone to come our way it's God, me, you and the family baby that's all that matter making you happy I love you boo always, since the first day I met you I have wanted you this is gone to happen baby okay.

Ms. Bossy are you getting everything together for us because I don't know how to plan a wedding whatever you do I'm sure I will be happy with it and find us the rings baby if it's not what you want now I will upgrade later because we doing this quick Ms. Bossy. Mrs. Lowes I like the sound of that you know I have not changed my mind you gone get a spanking if you keep playing around baby right on that red behind you hear me☺. I don't know what you mean talking about a new bae you better throw that want ad away because you are spoken for baby you hear me, I know what you need baby a good (X-rated thought) :) and me to baby. Where will we take our honeymoon at and just keep praying to the Lord about it and everything will be alright, what's up with you seem like you not trying to put Lowes on your name don't make me spank you now☺. Smiling faces when it comes to you and tell the kids I said hello.

Rainiee: Me being the woman that I am I let Trojan know what I feel and what I stand for what I will and will not do or take from anyone most of all how I love Jesus Christ, the Father Lord God. I told him how I love and how deep it goes to keep my man, that I'm not having any foolishness from any side chick or baby mommy's it's me or go your way they will respect me and I will respect them. I told him I'll be that lady in the street and that you know what in the sheets and a mother plus wife, this is not free got put a ring on it.

If you are reading this book I hope it reaches you before and in time to understanding what I'm saying about anyone can tell you things that will have your nose wide open and you won't listen to anyone else. I have had TKO's that was a mighty blow but I survived then I had if loving you is wrong I don't want to be right wrong was I and I was swimming because I got hurt by them lies. Now that I have had broken relationships I have learned what to watch for them RED FLAGS *that these are just words that cause me to fall if I keep listening*. The tone of the wording being spoken can tell you and the body gestures speaks loud you got to watch and listen because we have people out here that can talk the paint off the walls(just saying how smooth they can be). Do you want to be a king, queen or the concubine?

Who would not want to be swept off their feet and romanced to be the number one? I'm not gone to lie the brother got skills and only if I would have wrote all what he said to me you would be like way he at (laughing out loud). To that I'm so glad I got Jesus and the Holy Ghost living in me and keeping me because if I didn't I may have been shaking again and that's not what I'm going for. What do I believe for who do I stand for is got to be first in my life? That's why if you don't know what or who to watch out for it could end very sad. I ask you to be very careful please watch out.

Trojan: Hey Li-Mommy how are you doing I hope that you are doing well and in good health, baby what can I say after the last two letters like that for the first time in my life I'm at a loss for words and that don't happen to me. I had smiling faces all the way baby you show know how to make a man feel really good and I'm glad that I put a smile on your face all the time. I look at us and just am thankful that I have found a woman that's true to her word.

I just look back on all the things that I have been through, living a life of just wrong just about done everything up under the sun and what has it got me nothing? I wish people came with a warning sign subject to run up your credit subject to help send you to jail subject to beat up on you, so when you meet them you know what you getting see what I'm saying baby.

I truly believe when that man on TV said life is like a box of chocolate you never know what you are getting, you be taking chances to see what comes out of it but with you baby I'm willing to take it all. Because when you love someone as much as I love you we are together for the ups and downs in it and stand firm because the problem didn't bring us together love did. Money can't bring love it's for living to help pay bills and buy things don't let it tear you apart, I trust in God don't get me wrong I like money just don't let it define you.

Do you understand me baby? I'm not the richest man and I don't have everything nor do I have all the answers all I can do is trust God and wait on my blessings baby, have me a job if it's out there I'm gone to get it and take care of mines my queen and family. I do like having nice things and living good, God knows what I want and I know he can give it to me because I believe in his word ask and you shall receive.

I'm glad how you see me as man just smiling never had a woman to love me like you do and up lift her man, to stand by his side to build him up and not tear him down no matter what's wrong. A new love a new life with my Li-Mommy can't wait to hold you in my arms can't wait to look you in the eyes and tell you how much I love you can't wait to spend the rest of my life with you growing old together trying to make some babies☺. But any way I know that not happening Hu! But things gone to be alright baby your teddy bear is coming home soon to see what the Lord has plan for us. I hear you baby on everything you saying do your thing I'm sure you will be able to keep me from looking at them but you don't have to worry about that baby I only have eyes for you baby(X-rated thoughts).

Hey most beautiful how are you doing have anyone told you how beautiful you are today well I'm gone to tell you that every day and each day because you are inside and out You just don't find that much anymore in the world you know by the way have anyone said they love you I do baby I do with all my heart. Dame baby you got me hooked around here ☺ better to be hooked than sanked. Baby keep seeking God he is the only one that can help us keep praying for me baby keep me right.

I asked him a question about threesomes and like extra things to go in the bedroom because if he does I'm not the one for him because I don't swing that way. I like that he checked me on his answer letting me know I'm a man men don't go around asking the woman he wants to marry that I don't know what kind of guys you had before but I'm not him got me upset over here. Like you trying to get rid of me or something don't compare me to them I'm not them okay I Love you baby always have and always will Ms. Bossy with that crazy junk.

How can I love you and ask for another woman to join in with me and you in that moment that's special to me, woman you about to make me say some words you don't like. You are all the woman I need and I know how to spice things up where I don't need another person I got you don't I or am I reading you wrong baby? Unless you don't want me then it will take a long time to get over you, you are in my heart baby no one has ever been there except my mom you two are the ones I love that dear.

Yes I'm thinking back on this you will be the first woman I have asked to marry. It scares me sometimes how can I love someone this much and how I feel about you, I don't feel like humpy dumpy anymore I thought I would never feel like this again. You are my arm with fingers you are the blood that runs to my heart that makes it pump baby you just make me feel special, make me want to scream I'm in love to the world. When I close my eyes at night your face appears when I open my eyes in the morning your face appears when I think about you my heart skips a beat. I can't wait to be the man that do things for you that the other ones didn't do, your smile just to hold you and we do everything together that we have not done.

It's like we have been doing this for a long time and we just fine to begin because what we have is the truth there is no lies no misunderstanding in what we got. Baby you know you got me "dame I'm love struck" I'm I moving too fast because this is how I feel, you said I can tell you anything and I just ready to share my life with you. I feel I been alone my love for God never getting to where I suppose to be just feeling pain and you understand me and accept me for who I am that makes me love you even the more. I want to be the man that does right and live for God I know it can be done what more can a man ask for, you showed me that you are strong black woman that loves her man but God first.

Makes me happy to know you can keep things in order and you have a bossy side to you that will stand by my side. Hey baby, are you smiling today? Has God blessed you today? I pray for you and your family and things that are around you and I thought it was not possible for me to love again then you showed up and a light came on for me baby you was that light. Giving and taking goes on in this world not always good but was for me that you came in my life again, to have you in my arms as my wife, friend and lover and I would never give up on you or our Lord God. How is everything going for you in the church I hope it's going well for you and how is our family doing "yes" I said our family when we become one that makes them my family too. I'm not trying to replace anyone daddy but to become a father to them also because I love their mother and want nothing but the best for them and we be a happy family.

Rainiee: To point out if you are a single parent you don't want to bring everyone around your children if you don't know them that well and some children can pick up on that person evil side when you can't pick up on it so listen to them they want for you to be happy too. My daughter at the age of nine could since when a married came around me and she showed out made me think and observe more. And sometimes you can look people in the face to know if they are lying and sometimes they can fool you, we just need to be careful and by living in Gods kingdom we have protection. Power points to be protected by Gods almighty hand to be covered in the blood there's grace in his covering.

CHAPTER NINE

Trojan: I hear you on not letting people push me over the edge to get that mad, got to turn and cool down or just walk away from it to be an example in what I say I believe in. Well I tell you what's perfect is when two people get together and love one another through their problems and still love each other willing to take a chance with each other. The only outstanding perfect being is the Lord, that's just me baby who am I just a man looking for his soul mate. Baby I was yours before you even wrote the first letter you just didn't know it yet but now you do, I thank you for loving me for who I am and being who you are for your words of joy making me feel like Tarzan of the jungle.

Making me feel loved and wanted and I love you for that if this world was mines I would give you everything you wanted, you make me feel more than a man you make me want to conquer the world and give it to you. Something in my heart that's got me hooked on you will you marry me later baby [] yes [] no which one you pick and say? How you doing boo I hope you are feeling good and in good health and the family doing well have anyone told you they love you today? Well I will be the first to tell you I love you and that you are in my heart and I was thinking about what you said to take time to realize the little things in life.

Thinking about when you said to make love to the mind first then the body will come well I guess you have done that to me because you all in my mind☺. What I'm trying to say is we go good together "dame" I get goosebumps thinking about it sometimes I think it's a dream if it is don't wake me up I want to stay in this place with you. It's funny the only person I want to be around is you not just for sex or anything just to talk to you to be around you baby that's all, is that crazy baby for wanting that help me out here baby or am I hooked☺.

Baby I hear you about taking care of your man and you don't have to worry about me going anywhere I know you are a good woman and I'm lucky to have you. Baby you already give me a rush with your mind anything else is a blessing, yes it is amazing how God bring the right people in your life at the right time I'm proof of that you and Jesus. I hope you did good on your preaching naw I know you did well baby because that's what God want you to do right now. No one will ever think like you when God made you he didn't make another like you baby it's not you it's them baby always on your side till the end.

1. Will Trojan love wake sleeping beauty? you are already awake baby it just took the right one to come along if I have to kiss you a thousand times work a thousand jobs to wake you up I will you are beautiful.

2. Will Cinderella last past twelve midnight? We gone to last a lifetime baby this is just the beginning I got plenty of slippers for you in God.

3. Will this rainbow lead to the pot of gold? If you let it baby it's all up to you because I have found my gold in you know my diamond in you!

Layfayette Nicci Jackson-Steward

LOVE is like a firebomb when I hear your voice.

I know that you have been hurt so many times but baby you can't let that stop us from having what we have I will never hurt you baby you are in my heart boo! You will never have worry about me on God, God will always be in my heart always what is life without God nothing. Baby the words that I say are real I will never say nothing that I don't mean or say them just to get you I have not lied to you neither will I start now; all the words are from my heart. I will never do that because I have been done like that before and I didn't like it I'm here until you say that you don't want me no more.

I will always be there for you don't you know my queen my heart my friend, you took a man who thought love was impossible and made him live again. Made me know love is not impossible so baby me and you forever I'm glad you letting your wall down sorry you been hurt so many times, I just want to make that go away and that's the truth. When you hurt I hurt too dame you got me hooked☺ got me over here wanting to find every guy that hurt you and beat they a**, when you said you like to make mind love you wasn't lying. Just want to see how far we can go to the moon the stars and beyond baby all I ask is that you let me in and show you what real love is, a love that will never end a love from a person that truly respect you. It's not about the sex or what you got it's about the friendship that goes beyond sex baby.

It's to the point I thought a guy was talking about you and I was ready to fight this guy over it and that's when I knew you had me hooked because I was ready to fight. I'm like I know I care for this young lady but anyway baby I was jealous am I crazy baby. I only want to share you with God and your kids that's all ☺it's only because I love hard and maybe a little jealous at times that's all. I know that I want to take our relationship to the next level and it's funny how you ask me about how I rate love, over goes beyond any scale love can make you do crazy things. When you finish each other sentences that's where I want me and you to be at so I can put that ring on your finger but I know that's gone to take time I'm willing to wait for. I just don't want to see you sad or cry anymore so if you give me a chance to make you happy.

Rainiee: It's getting to the end and time is getting closer for me and Trojan to meet up. I asked him do he have a temper that I need to know about and I see where his tone and writing is starting to change up, asking myself what is going on is this just a dream for me and just words being told to me for what is this another liar I have meet?

Trojan: I'm a man that will not put his hands on a woman like that I will leave first plus a man should know how to control himself and remove to void any predicaments of that nature. Oh yeah that name of yours will be changed in the near future Mrs. Lowes has a good sound to it. But my plans for life is to try and serve God as best as I can to build a future with you the woman I love, work and take care of our family. To do for you what no other has.

Rainiee: Well folks this was the last letter and phone call I received from Trojan the seventh of January two thousand and fifteen and we started talking in August of two thousand and fourteen. After all the "I love you" and "I will never lie" or "hurt you" I'm a real man to my word. I asked God to give me a sign if this the husband you have for me before I get my feelings involved it looked closed but no it wasn't it. We can't want love that bad that we settle for anything or be in denial to the truth. I was ready after the fact how the brother was talking ready to get my engine burning you hear me!

Key point I was not gone to compromise myself anymore for this flesh, my Bible tells me what I use to do is passed away and all things become new and I must present my body a living sacrifice, holy, acceptable unto God, which is your reasonable service (2 Corinthians 5 Romans 12).

That's why if I'm not your wife and you want to keep bringing up sex and not God it's time for me to leave because that's what you are after.

To all my readers I pray that this really helps and bless you. What made me was my past preparing me for jokers like this the fake coming before the real deal.

It's funny how they say they want a "dime shaped figure and they not even a seven, eight or a nine".

Baby I'm here to tell you what the Lord Almighty God says about me, He loves me beyond what I can think. Jesus died and rose on the third day with all power in "HIS HAND" to be seated on the right side of his Father. Be still my child and wait on me to move for you

(Psalm 46:10; 28:7). And, behold, I am with thee, and will keep thee in all places whither thou goest, and will bring thee again into this land; for I will not leave thee, until I have done that which I have spoken to thee of(Genesis28:15).

I gave myself to God and when my ex-left I thought I needed a man to be there to comfort me, when I stepped out into my mess of sin it was a bondage I open the door to. In the mist of me wanting some man company to fill the itch I was having turned out to be the worst time I had, when you belong to God you just can't do anything you want to, say, go or dress anyway (well that applies to me I don't know about you).

Learning that my wants are not God wants for me so I need to seek God wants for my life first. When I had sinned it made me feel so disgusting and hating to look at him, had me feeling like I lost the only thing that matter to me and that was Jesus I repented from it. This time I know to hear from God before I do anything and to put this flesh to death because I was in the middle of the ocean without a life jacket when I walked in self.

Do you really want God to allow what you want to come? We reject his will to do what we want to do which will become a lesson until we repent, we have disobeyed Him and disobedience brings on judgment (Revelation 3:19).

Now I can listen to my Father to know who's a fake or just trying to fill my head up with bull crap I don't need.

You can't always wait for someone to come your way when you're down so you better know how to pray your way out of your mess. Give God praise for keeping His hands on you.

You can't get caught up in man because when they hurt you to no point of return what you gone do then? If you take the time out to know Jesus first to learn a person before you go pass wait and jump directly to bedroom or birthday sex, then you can keep the spare tires for your car because I can buy my own drink thank you.

help me and you understand how you want change for yourself if you keep going the same dead-end route, you looking for the wrong light its' not at motel 6. I have learned I gave my love away to some that didn't even care thinking that it meant something to you, now I have to forgive you and let go so I can grow. To anyone I gave that just thrashed my love I gave to you.

I'm not the CDs to your DVD player that you turn on at will, because I didn't let you score as if I was one of your seasons games now it's game over you on to the next victim. Tell it like it is if you give up the butt the first night all you will be is a fly by night booty call unless you are Sunshine from Harlem Nights. Lot of us doesn't know how to love give love or receive love leaving us to look in the wrong places or things rushing before we learn anything. Don't let anyone pull you down to the dark side of what they are doing when you are learning the truth and make you feel less than because you didn't fall into their trap.

LIPS OF FIRE

Now I'm just avoid to you, you can't say you love me and beat, call me names or belittle me I thought it was me never knew joy until you left. Been there so many times now I'm watching the tides roll away each time with a piece of my old pains, tears, hurts, worries and scares as the new waves come back to refill me a new (Ecclesiastes 3). God is everything when you need Him the most when you slow down and stop God will let you laugh at things when you don't need to cry. Remind yourself don't love anyone more than you love God.

No matter what God Is God.

Even when you feel below dirt God Is.

How people treat you God Is.

The very smile on your face, the tears in your eyes, God Is God.

In my words stop it I say!

I hear people always saying how fine someone is oh that shape is off the maps and I never hear them say what are the goals of that person for their life or what are their plans for life? To me they want a coca-cola shape woman or muscle man. You have to bring more to the table than just sex or a nice figure! Cooking, cleaning, preparing (work) and savings (building together) and love beyond the body.

FINAL THOUGHTS AND NUGGETS

My main goal is to let people know that we must hold on to God no matter what. He will direct our path to the end. We must stand on our faith if we are single. Love it until God changes it. We must seek his face first in all we do. It's not always sunshine but God, I failed before and now I'm stronger. I now know when God is telling me to go, turn, run, stand and roll over.

No matter what age if God knocks answer him before the world knocks at you. It may be times you are feeling all alone but God is there to lean on him.

Have you seen & heard the saying how the young is lost running around not listening just full of specimen & the old just full of worms trying to be young. Some folks are spared with just a STD and others get full blown Aids and don't live long. All because you want to do what you want, sleeping with any & everybody without condoms. Playing with the devil he will take you further than you want to go and keep you longer than you want to stay. I won't lie somethings we do we like a lot but it is not worth dying & going to hell for! Sex we like a lot but it is so much better with one husband & one wife together covered by God. Don't be in sin & let the glimmer-hype fool you to think it's more and only be three minutes and now you feel dirty & ashamed. It will have you missing God if you are saved, crying for him to come back in your life. Read Luke 15 the prodigal son. His presence don't always come back quick in your life then you feeling like a cactus without water, a dry tumbleweed with no wind. I know I'm not jacked up truth be told I'm just backed up I know the difference. I will be thou Holy just as the Lord is Holy, meaning I'm single and waiting on the Lord and I'm not bored or unhappy living this life for God. People can say what they want I don't care because they have no heaven or hell to put me in. So am not gone to let you keep me from heaven this heat here is close enough to hell for me. Hell can keep its reservation I'm no longer available I'm sold out to Jesus fully committed to serving him. I thank God for my children (James, uncle RayRay & Naenae & my G-baby Chole aka Ms. Pepper Jack, my son Brain & my Ashley F, Dada L-W, Tete& Rere M, Tez, Shasha & Aj R. They have helped me and kept me young.

ABOUT THE AUTHOR

LayFayette "Nicci" Jackson-Steward is a native of Jacksonville, Florida. She is a loving mother and grandmother. She is active in her church and community. This is her second published work.

Printed in Great Britain
by Amazon